Living in
God's Will

Living in God's Will

STONECROFT

HARVEST HOUSE PUBLISHERS
EUGENE, OREGON

Cover by Koechel Peterson & Associates, Inc., Minneapolis, Minnesota
Cover photo © Goodshoot / Thinkstock

LIVING IN GOD'S WILL
Stonecroft Bible Studies
Copyright © 2013 by Stonecroft Ministries, Inc.
Published by Harvest House Publishers
Eugene, Oregon 97402
www.harvesthousepublishers.com

ISBN 978-0-7369-5266-8 (pbk.)
ISBN 978-0-7369-5267-5 (eBook)

Contents

|||||||||||||||||||||||||||||||||

Welcome to Stonecroft Bible Studies!   7

1. Can We Know God's Will? *(Ruth 1:1-2)*   9
2. Right Motive—Wrong Decision *(Ruth 1:1-13)* 21
3. Ruth's Decision *(Ruth 1:14-22)* 39
4. Israel's Custom *(Ruth 2:1-16)* 53
5. A New Beginning *(Ruth 2:17-23)* 65
6. Ruth's Request *(Ruth 3:1-18)* 79
7. The Result of Right Decisions *(Ruth 4:1-22)* 93

Journal Pages 105
Know God 113
Who Is Stonecroft? 117
Books for Further Study 119
Stonecroft Resources 121
Notes 127

Acknowledgments

Stonecroft wishes to acknowledge and thank Janice Mayo Mathers for her dedication in serving the Lord through Stonecroft. Speaker, author, and member of the Board of Directors, Jan is the primary author of revised Stonecroft Bible Studies. We appreciate her love for God's Word and her love for people who need Him. Stonecroft also thanks the team who prayed for Jan, and those who edited, designed, and offered their creative input to make these studies accessible to all.

Welcome to
Stonecroft Bible Studies!

At Stonecroft, we connect you with God, each other, and your communities.

It doesn't matter where you've been or what you've done—God wants to be in relationship with you. And one place He tells you about Himself is in His Word—the Bible. Whether the Bible is familiar or new to you, its contents will transform your life and bring answers to your biggest questions.

Gather with people in your communities—women, men, couples, young and old alike—and find out together what the Bible's book of Ruth has to say about discovering God's will for you. Follow Ruth and her mother-in-law, Naomi, through the hard times of their lives and see how they respond to God in their choices—and what He brings about for their future. You will discover how their lives point the way for you as you learn to trust God for your own decisions in life.

Each chapter of *Living in God's Will* includes discussion questions to stir up meaningful conversation, specific Scripture verses to investigate, and time for prayer to connect with God and each other.

Discover more of God and His ways through this small-group exploration of the Bible.

Tips for Using This Study

This book has several features that make it easy to use and helpful for your life:

- The page number or numbers given after every Bible reference are keyed to the page numbers in the *Abundant Life Bible*. This handy paperback Bible uses the New Living Translation, a recent version in straightforward, up-to-date language. We encourage you to obtain a copy through your group leader or at stonecroft.org.

- Each chapter ends with a section called "Thoughts, Notes, and Prayer Requests." Use this space for notes or for thoughts that come to you during your group time or study, as well as prayer requests.

- In the back of the book you will find "Journal Pages"—a space available for writing down how the study is changing your life or any other personal thoughts, reactions, and reflections.

- Please make this book and study your own. We encourage you to use it and mark it in any way that helps you grow in your relationship with God!

If you find this study helpful, you may want to investigate other resources from Stonecroft Ministries. Please take a look at "Stonecroft Resources" in the back of the book or online at **stonecroft.org/store**.

stonecroft.org

1

Can We Know God's Will?
Ruth 1:1-2

I decided it was time to move! Since I was young and single, my decision didn't rock anyone's world. My family just shook their heads, wondering if I'd ever settle down. With my car loaded up, I headed toward my new city of choice. On the way, I decided to take a quick side trip to visit a friend. She and her fiancé arranged an evening out for us, and the fiancé brought along his roommate to even up the number.

And just like that, my wandering days came to an end. Two days later I'd found a job and unpacked my belongings in my friend's spare room. Thirty-eight years later I'm still married to the roommate. Who knew that last-minute decision would lead to a life-altering journey?

Prayer

Lord, thank you that anytime I need wisdom, I just have to ask you, and you will give it to me. You will not correct me for asking. Thank you too for promising to guide me along the best path for my life. I know that you will advise me and watch over me (James 1:5, page 930, and Psalm 32:8, page 427).

Can We Know God's Will?

If only our foresight were as good as our hindsight! Life would be much easier, wouldn't it? We wouldn't have to worry about whether or not we're making the right decision. We can spend days, weeks, even months, agonizing over major decisions, and then a small, insignificant choice we make—such as a side trip to visit a friend—will significantly alter our lives.

One thing is certain. Every decision we make, big or small, does impact our life. Some decisions enhance our lives, some detract, but they all combine to make our lives what they are today.

What are some significant choices you have made that have impacted your life, both positively and negatively?

What are some *insignificant* choices you have made that have impacted your life?

A common mistake we make is thinking that our decisions only affect us. This couldn't be further from the truth. Every choice—good or bad, big or little—can have ripple effects in the lives of those around us.

Sometimes the decision we are facing is clear. We instinctively know what is best. Sometimes, though, it is not so clear. Details and possible outcomes complicate it, making objectivity impossible. Our personal desire gets in the way…or what seems reasonable does not line up with what seems wise.

Here is the truth: Choices guided by our human way of thinking will result in human decisions. That's not a big deal when we're deciding between apple pie or chocolate cake. But when lives are involved, it becomes a much bigger deal.

What does Proverbs 14:12 (page 490) say?

Have you ever been so sure you were making the right decision, only to have it blow up in your face? What did you learn from that experience?

It is so important to make God a part of our decision-making process. We don't have the advantage of foresight, *but He does,* and He has offered us access to His unlimited wisdom. He is omniscient, which means He has complete and unlimited knowledge, awareness, and understanding. Can you see why accessing His omniscience would be a huge advantage in the decision-making process?

How are God's thoughts different from our thoughts, according to Isaiah 55:8-9 (page 560)?

God will bring things to our mind that we would never consider. He will expand our thinking and broaden our insight to equip us to make the right decision. The wonderful thing to know is that as long as your heart continues to beat, you can make better choices. While some doors may be forever closed because of past decisions, you can still make decisions now that will result in a satisfying, purposeful life that brings glory to God.

But how do we access God's wisdom so we can know what the best decision is? You have already taken the first step by choosing to participate in this study. You are in for a treat as, over these seven chapters, we learn the key principles in discerning God's will for our lives.

A good book for this purpose is the book of Ruth in the Old Testament, and I promise you are going to *love* this book. It is riveting from start to finish.

The Background of the Book of Ruth

Ruth is one of only two books in the Bible named after women. The other book, Esther, is about a young Jewish woman who became queen of the Persian Empire and was used by God to save her people from extinction. Ruth is about a young Moabite woman who also followed God's lead—right smack into the earthly lineage of Jesus Christ! Both of these women are outstanding examples of what happens when you involve God in the decision-making process.

The book of Ruth has only 4 chapters (85 verses total), but it is jam-packed with profound life lessons that are applicable to us today. It is a true story woven around the choices of at least eight people. And it takes place during a very dark period of Israel's history, known as the Time of the Judges. This period came after the Israelites had settled in the land of Canaan—the "Promised Land"—and before the reign of the kings began.

To briefly recap the history leading up to this time, Moses led the Israelites out of slavery in Egypt. He was God's appointed leader over them, both politically and spiritually, through the 40 years they wandered in the desert after refusing to believe God and obey His direction to enter the land He had promised would be theirs.

After Moses' death and the death of the unbelieving generation of Israelites, God appointed Joshua to be their leader, and under his guidance Israel at last went into the Promised Land. In time, the land was divided up among their 12 tribes, and each tribe lived on their own land. Joshua was dead by then, and they no longer had a human spiritual leader—instead, God was their spiritual leader.

What follows is a sad but familiar story. Similar ones continue to take place even today. The Israelites chose not to follow God's lead. They settled among the Canaanites and adopted many of their heathen ways. Read Judges 2:1-2 (page 189).

God eventually appointed judges for Israel, but the nation as a whole continued to be apathetic toward God. They failed to teach their children about Him, so a whole generation grew up in spiritual ignorance. A line that appears a couple times in the book of Judges describes their philosophy at the time. Read Judges 17:6 (page 203). Who dictated what the people did?

This philosophy cropped up many times in both the Old and New Testament. It is actually the mindset of today's culture. What is the danger of practicing this philosophy?

This was a period of tremendous unrest for the Israelites that resulted in crime, tribal jealousy, wars, immorality, violence, and oppression by foreign nations. They not only turned their backs on the true God, but they went so far as to embrace other gods and worship idols made of wood, metal, or stone. They had no moral strength to make wise choices and life became miserable for them. Things would get into such an unbearable state that they would finally cry out to God for help.

As He always does, God would answer them. He would choose a judge to lead them. This enabled them to fight back against the enemy nations that were oppressing them. Back in alignment with God, their situation improved as He blessed them.

Then, in their prosperity, they would begin to ignore Him again, spiraling back down to *"doing whatever seemed right in their own eyes."* It was a depressing, completely avoidable cycle. During approximately 400 years of judges, the Israelites spent more than 90 years in captivity!

It is during this period of time (12 centuries before the birth of Christ) that the events in the book of Ruth unfold. Although it takes place during the time of the judges, the book was probably not written until after David became king of Israel. The biggest indication of this is that the last two verses of the book give a brief genealogy. Read Ruth 4:21-22 (page 210).

Since the genealogy does not mention Solomon, David's son who became king after him, we can assume that it was written before Solomon's reign. The most wonderful aspect of the book of Ruth is that it clearly shows the sovereignty of God. Even in the midst of cold spiritual hearts and lousy decisions, He continued to work behind the scenes to bring about His perfect will.

Okay, enough background! Let's get started.

The Choices of Elimelech and Naomi

Read Ruth 1:1-2 (page 208).

Why did Elimelech leave Bethlehem?

Where did Elimelech move his family to?

Most likely, we have all seen images of famine-stricken countries. What images does the phrase *severe famine* bring to your mind? It's a gut-wrenching sight, but it is with those images that the story begins.

We do not know why there was a famine. Different degrees of famine happen all over the world. But the famine referred to in Ruth was an instance where the land wasn't producing enough food to feed its people, probably due to insufficient rainfall.

God communicates to us in times of blessing and in times of heartache—always seeking to draw us into relationship with Him. One of His most wonderful tools of communication is the Bible—His inspired Word to us. It shows us His love and teaches us about His trustworthy character, no matter what circumstances we find ourselves facing in this life. Read the following verses and note what they say.

Job 1:21 (page 390)

Psalm 37:25 (page 430)

What is your reaction to these verses?

Naomi and Elimelech would have known of the repeated inter-vention and protection God gave to their ancestors while wander-ing through the desert—40 years of food they never had to grow for themselves, 40 years of clothes and shoes that never wore out, water gushing from a rock to quench their thirst. They had plenty of evi-dence of God's ability to protect His followers. You can read the story yourself in Exodus 15–17 (pages 55-58).

We don't know how long the famine had been going on, so we do not know how bad the circumstances were—whether this was a pre-emptive move on the family's part or a last-resort move. We just know their level of concern was such they were willing to leave their home-land, their means of income, their family and friends—everything near and dear—to move to a foreign land.

Depending on the route they took, it would have been a seven-to-ten-day journey on foot through steep and rugged country. It's not likely they made the decision to move on the spur of the moment. More likely, Elimelech and Naomi labored long and hard over this decision, because this wasn't just any country they were moving to—this was Moab.

But they were two people just like you and me, who were trying to take care of their family. When the famine took hold they probably began to get nervous. They were focusing on the circumstances facing them instead of God, and their decision-making ability became impaired. They decided to do *"what was right in their own eyes"*. They would have been better off staying in the Promised Land than immigrating to Moab.

Read Deuteronomy 23:3-6 (page 156).

Why shouldn't Elimelech's and Naomi's family have moved to Moab?

Where they moved is telling—it shows their desperation as well as their broken communication with God, because the family left the land that God had given them (Exodus 6:4, page 47).

The Moabites were long-time enemies of the Israelites. Chapters 22 through 25 of the book of Numbers (pages 124-127) tell how the Moabites tried to keep the Israelites from entering the land God had promised them by hiring someone to put a curse on them. Instead of reading all those chapters, let's read the summary of this event in Joshua 24:9-10 (page 186).

The Moabites had devised their own religion based on a made-up god they called Chemosh. This religion was a despicable one, requiring atrocities from the people—including the sacrifice of their own children.

Considering Our Own Decisions

From the warmth and comfort of our homes, centuries later, it is easy to pass judgment. Their family was exactly where they were supposed to be—living in the land God had promised them. *How could Elimelech and Naomi turn away from God and move their children to a culture like that?* Place yourself in their shoes for a moment. You are in the midst of a terrible famine and you have two growing boys to feed. It is easy to misinterpret what our most pressing needs are when we are in the middle of a devastating storm and we fail to remember what God has promised us.

Think of an example where you or someone you know made a decision rooted in emotions rather than in the promises of God. What was the result?

We have all made "in the moment" decisions. Our first instinct is emotional, but what we need to keep in mind is that our knowledge is limited to past experiences and present circumstances. God's knowledge includes all of the past, present, and future. Learning to discern His guidance will always lead us in the right direction.

Before we finish this chapter, if you want to know what God's will is in regard to an aspect of your life or a decision you are facing, write what the situation is in the space below.

What are the possible options or solutions?

We'll come back to these notes at the end of the study and see if you have gained any insight or knowledge that will help in your decision.

———— *Personal Reflection and Application* ————

From this chapter,

I see...

I believe...

I will...

Prayer

Lord, how grateful I am that you help me to hear you. From right behind me I hear your voice saying, "This is the way you should go," whether to the right or to the left. You have promised to guide me along the best pathway for my life. You have promised to advise me and watch over me (Isaiah 30:21, pages 539-540, and Psalm 32:8, page 427).

Thoughts, Notes, and Prayer Requests

2

Right Motive—Wrong Decision
Ruth 1:1-13

Ira Yates was a rancher who lived in West Texas during the 1920s. His land, the "River Ranch," was poor, and he struggled to get ahead financially.

Eventually Yates came up with the idea of getting an oil company to drill on his ranch, even though everyone considered the land worthless. He convinced one of the companies to sign a lease contract with him. On the fourth well they drilled, at just over 1000 feet deep, they struck an immense oil reserve. The well produced 80,000 barrels a day! Subsequent wells were also profitable. *And Mr. Yates owned it all.* All that time he'd been struggling, he was actually a multimillionaire. He just didn't know it.[1]

Prayer

Lord, how wonderful to know that you direct my steps and you delight in every detail of my life. Thank you for giving me your Word to be a lamp to guide my feet and a light for my path (Psalm 37:23, page 430, and Psalm 119:105, page 470).

Elimelech is a good example of a millionaire who was living like a pauper, thinking like a pauper. Worried about the famine and not knowing how long it would last or how his family would survive, he took matters into his own hands rather than access the unlimited resources God had made available to him. He made his decision from the perspective of human probability rather than God's possibilities. His motives were right, but his decision was wrong—and we've all been there at one time or another. And while the Bible doesn't say whether Elimelech and his family prospered in Moab, we do know that God was specific about avoiding that region, and He should have been obeyed.

Have you ever wondered what people mean when they talk about finding God's will or praying for His will? God's will actually takes the blame for a lot of things that result from our own human will. Can you think of an example of this?

When we talk about God's will, we often separate it into three aspects. There is His sovereign will, His moral will, and His will for the individual. Let's look at each of these.

The Sovereign Will of God

God's sovereign will refers to His perfect plan for the entire universe and all of time. His sovereign will cannot be changed.

Prophecy is a part of God's sovereign will. All that He has prophesied will be fulfilled. Read Isaiah 46:10 (page 554).

The birth, death, and resurrection of Jesus are examples of God's sovereign will that were prophesied in Scripture and have already occurred. Jesus' future return to earth is an example of God's sovereign will that has been prophesied but has not yet occurred. We have no control over biblically prophesied events. They are part of His sovereign will.

How God's sovereign will and our individual will fit together is a mystery known only to Him. We are each responsible for every decision we make. God does not violate our will or take away our decision-making ability.

The Moral Will of God

The Bible tells us everything we need to know about God's moral will. It tells us what we need to know to live a purposeful life that pleases Him. The Ten Commandments are an example of His moral will. You can find them in their entirety in Exodus 20:2-17 (page 59), but Jesus summed them up in Matthew 22:37-39 (page 753). What does it say?

Two other examples of God's moral will are found in the following verses:

2 Corinthians 6:14-15 (page 885)
1 Thessalonians 4:3 (page 906)

Considering these verses, what do you think God's motive was for establishing these two moral codes?

The purpose of God's moral will is not to limit our lives, but to enhance them. When we go against His moral will, our life will begin to develop limitations—emotionally, mentally, physically, and spiritually. What are some limitations that might develop from going against the two aspects of His moral will that are mentioned in the verses we just read?

Some more examples of God's moral law are found in the following verses. As you read, make a list of what they tell us to do.

Philippians 4:5-9 (page 901)

1 Thessalonians 5:16-22 (page 907)

Look over the list you made. Which items or concepts are repeated?

Did you notice how most of them have to do with having the right mindset? Regardless of what circumstances come into our life, we need to set our mind *beforehand* to act considerately to all involved— to not worry, to pray always, to be thankful, to think good and true thoughts, and to be joyful. This is where our free will comes in. God doesn't force us to follow His moral law. Because of the freedom He has given us, we decide what aspects of it we will or will not follow. However, choosing to follow His moral guidelines will enhance our relationship with Him.

These same guidelines that God has set in 1 Thessalonians were also mentioned in Philippians. Read Philippians 4:4-9 again (page 901). What will we receive when we incorporate these into our lives?

One of the most significant losses that results from going against God's moral law is the loss of our peace of mind. When we feel anxiety building within us that's not related to circumstances beyond our control, chances are it is related to a behavior or attitude that is in opposition to God's moral law. Can you think of an example of this in your personal or professional life?

Following God's moral law guarantees we will experience peace, no matter how stormy things get. The best way to know His moral will is to become intimately familiar with His Word—the Bible.

God's Will for Us as Individuals

The third aspect of God's will has to do with individual choices we make. For example, when choosing a spouse, His moral will says that as a Christ-follower, we should choose someone who also follows Christ—but it doesn't say *which* follower to choose. That's an individual choice we make. Finding the individual will of God for our lives is what this study is about.

God has a plan for each of us. He guides us in His plan through the indwelling Holy Spirit, as we make daily decisions. Another way to look at it is receiving the guidance we need day by day. We can pray with the psalmist, *"Teach me to do your will, for you are my God. May your gracious Spirit lead me forward on a firm footing"* (Psalm 143:10, page 478).

Read the following verses. What do they tell you about finding God's will?

Proverbs 16:9 (page 492)

Psalm 37:23 (page 430)

If we are living within God's moral will, He will direct our steps as we make our plans, because He delights in every detail of our lives!

The Bible gives plenty of guidelines that are helpful when determining God's will in various circumstances. Read the following verses and note what they say.

James 1:5 (page 930)

How can we gain God's wisdom?

What criteria would you use to assess whether something is from God's wisdom or from ours?

In what ways could we misuse God's wisdom in discerning His will?

One way to know that it is God's wisdom we are following is by seeing if it agrees with His whole moral will as revealed in His Word.

The more acquainted we are with God and His Word, which is absolutely trustworthy, the less likely we are to make the wrong decision. This has practical applications in how we treat people.

Now read Proverbs 15:22 (page 491).

How do you see this as being to your advantage?

Read Psalm 37:4 (page 429).

Isn't that great? When we delight in God, He will give us the desires of our hearts. How do we delight in Him?

God does not just give us everything we desire whether it's good or bad. When we delight in Him—spending time with Him, enjoying His presence, meditating on His Word, and so on—our heart's desires will shift and closely align themselves with His desires.

If you are His child, living in the Spirit and being obedient to God, then your decisions will be in His will.

Read Romans 8:28-29 (page 863).

God may not allow us to see His "good reasons" for the way things turn out. Sometimes He does let us see them. We must not insist on some justification that satisfies us. He is not obligated to explain Himself. If we trust in Him, we will believe that things fit into a pattern of good, even if human evidence seems otherwise.

There is beauty in our relationship with God. Human mistakes are

> "The discipline of discerning His voice really boils down to one very simple yet poignant principle: The more you *know* God, the more clearly you can *hear* God."
>
> —Priscilla Shirer

inevitable. Sometimes, with the best of intentions, we make the wrong decision. God does not abandon us in these decisions. Instead, if we let Him, He will work with us to obtain a good outcome. And in the process He continues to make us more like Christ.

This can be seen in the book of Ruth: God took Elimelech's poor decision, made out of concern for his family, and turned it around for His glory.

Granted, we know very little about Elimelech, but what parts of God's will do you see him ignoring?

A Great Sorrow Comes

Read Ruth 1:3-5 (page 208).

In a mere 51 words, a time of great sorrow is summed up with clinical dispassion. So many facts are left out. How long were they in Moab before Elimelech died? Had they achieved better circumstances? Were their stomachs once again full? Had they established a means of support? We just don't know. We only know that in escaping the physical famine in Bethlehem, they encountered an emotional famine of much greater magnitude in Moab.

With so many details left out, it is easy to try to read between the lines and fill in a few possible details.

Most likely, the family went to Moab with the intention of only riding out the famine. But they ended up settling there—and soon ten years had passed. Don't forget the vast difference between Israelite and Moabite cultures. Don't forget they are living among their enemies. And yet they stayed there for ten years.

This isn't so surprising, though, when you think about it. Take a minute and reflect on your own experience. Think of a time when you compromised something you knew you shouldn't have. Once that compromise was made, was it easier to make even more compromises thereafter? It is shocking how quickly we grow to accept different habits or philosophies the further we are immersed into another context. When we choose to go a different way than God is leading, there is always the danger of staying away longer than we planned and going further than we intended. We do not know how long the family originally wanted to stay in Moab, but we do know that they lived there for around ten years. Most likely it was a longer stay than they had initially planned.

Finding herself a widow in the land of Moab, Naomi chose to remain there with her sons rather than return to her homeland and the support of her people.

What do you think some of her reasons for staying might have been?

Regardless of her reasons, exactly what you would expect to happen did. Her sons married Moabite women. This showed blatant disregard on several levels for what God had told the Israelites. He'd told them to have nothing to do with the Moabites and that no Moabite, nor their children to the tenth generation, was allowed to enter the place of worship. Read Deuteronomy 23:3 (page 156). Naomi chose not only to continue living among the Moabites, but now both her sons had intermarried with them.

What thoughts do you suppose ran through Naomi's head when she lay down to sleep at night? How many tears do you think she shed as she surveyed the shape her life had taken? Single women were so vulnerable in that culture. Did she worry over how she would survive in Moab without a husband to protect her? Did she worry about going against God's express will? The mounting toll of compromise was staggering.

Do you think she ever asked God why? *Why did you let the famine come? Why did you let my husband die? Why have you turned your back on me?*

Have you ever asked God the same kind of questions about your own circumstances?

In spite of her concerns, the possibility of grandchildren must have given Naomi great hope. A grandson would carry on Elimelech's name, which was of ultimate importance in ancient cultures. It would also secure her own future, giving her someone who would care for and protect her in her old age. But neither daughter-in-law conceived before their husbands died.

If you've experienced infertility, you know precisely how long several years is when you have your hopes dashed month after agonizing month. It was an endless, unbearable heartache for Naomi's daughters-in-law, made much worse by the fact that an inability to bear children in ancient cultures was an immense failure and disgrace. A woman's main purpose was to bear children, preferably sons.

Still this battered little family had not reached the end of its loss. The absolute worst happens when not just one of Naomi's sons dies—*both* die. Suddenly Naomi is alone with her two foreign daughters-in-law, facing as hopeless a future as one can imagine. In her book *The Gospel of Ruth*, Carolyn Custis James compares Naomi's plight to that of Job (pages 390-414). You may recall that Job went down in history for the depth of his suffering: losing his children, his health, his wealth, and his livelihood. James contends Naomi's suffering was even worse. "Both," she says, "tragically lose their families and the life they worked to build. But Job is not alone. He still has his wife and a community to surround him (such as they are). Job is not an immigrant and he is not a woman."[2]

James is right. Being a woman in ancient times did not work to one's advantage. Naomi and her two daughters-in-law were highly vulnerable in that male-dominated culture.

Have you ever found yourself thrust into circumstances more painful or fearful than you thought you could bear? What emotions did you struggle with?

What was your response?

Read verses 6-13 (page 208).

What emotions did Naomi struggle with in verse 13?

What was her response?

Naomi's words to her grieving daughters-in-law in the last half of verse 13 are telling. She had become so focused on all she had suffered that she was unable to see beyond her own pain. She knew God, yet she refused to turn toward His promised comfort and instead blamed Him for what had happened.

Have you ever blamed God for circumstances in your life?

How did it affect your relationship with Him?

The circumstances that caused you to blame God can either draw you closer to Him or create barriers between you and Him. Take great care—other people may offer temporary comfort, but only God can provide a lasting peace and comfort when we turn to Him in our pain. Will you allow Him to reveal Himself to you in this situation?

The Three Women's Choices

While we have no control over the circumstances that blow into our lives, what do we have absolute control of?

In his book *Man's Search for Meaning*, psychologist Viktor Frankl recounts his experiences as an inmate of Hitler's notorious concentration camps. He observed that although every prisoner suffered the same incomprehensible atrocities, some managed to hold on to their "self" better than others. He said it became clear to him "that the sort of person the prisoner became was the result of an inner decision" and not the result of their outer circumstances.[3]

Today we may not be able to relate to the torture of imprisonment, but we can learn from this very painful experience—and the response they had in the midst of it.

The Bible is filled with promises to enable us to make the kind of inner decisions that will help us hold on to our "self" regardless of our circumstances. One such passage is Romans 8:35-39 (page 863).

What does verse 37 say is ours, no matter what is happening?

Not just victory, but *"overwhelming victory"*! What do verses 38 and 39 say can separate us from God's love?

It would be interesting to know what Orpah's and Ruth's internal response was to their mother-in-law's statement. Perhaps it didn't even register because their minds were reeling even more over something else Naomi had just said to them. Remember, these two young women have chosen to leave their homeland and follow their mother-in-law back to her country. These two childless widows have packed up their belongings and said goodbye to all they have ever known. In Israel they would have no one to protect them, care for them, or even love them except their grief-stricken, bitter mother-in-law. They are on their way to Bethlehem, when suddenly Naomi stops and turns to them.

What does she tell them in Ruth 1:8-9 (page 208)?

What difficult words to come from Naomi's lips. Why do you think she encouraged her daughters-in-law to go back?

One reason could have been pride. Returning to her homeland with two foreign daughters-in-law in tow would have been proof of just how far Naomi had strayed in her relationship with God. Perhaps she couldn't bear the thought of hearing "I told you so" from people who'd warned her of that very possibility when she and her husband took their single sons to live among their enemies. Perhaps it was simply that she knew it would be easier for Ruth and Orpah to get on with their lives in their home country.

According to verse 10, what is the young women's response to Naomi's words?

There is no way of knowing for sure, but their willingness to go with Naomi and live among her people makes you wonder what life was like for them in Moab. In a culture where marriages were arranged to benefit families, what father would have found benefit in arranging a marriage between his daughter and a foreigner from an enemy country? Beyond that, were the young women socially ostracized for marrying foreigners? Whatever the truth might have been, one thing is certain: From a human standpoint their future looked grim indeed.

Verses 11 and 12 reveal Naomi's misguided logic and show that perhaps her motives weren't selfish in sending the women back to their home. What does she tell them?

When Naomi spoke about not having other sons for them to marry, she was speaking about a Jewish custom by which the brother of the man who died childless would marry the widow in order to conceive a son to carry on the dead man's inheritance. This Jewish custom is explained in Deuteronomy 25:5-6 (page 158).

Naomi's sons were both dead, however. She had no source of hope to offer the young women. Marriage and giving birth to sons were a woman's only hope for security. Perhaps she was thinking in those terms when telling them to return. Nonetheless, her instruction is the result of a thought process that has left God out of the equation.

So here the three women stand at a crossroads, with life-altering decisions to be made. Naomi has made hers—she's returning home now that the famine has ended (verse 6), and is willing to go alone. What decision will her daughters-in-law make?

We'll find out in the next chapter!

─────── *Personal Reflection and Application* ───────

From this chapter,

I see...

I believe...

I will...

─────── ⤳⤲ ───────

Prayer

Lord, help me to pay attention to what you say and to listen carefully to your words. Don't let me lose sight of them. Let them penetrate deep into my heart, so they can bring life to me and healing for my whole body (Proverbs 4:20-22, page 483).

─────── *Thoughts, Notes, and Prayer Requests* ───────

_____

_____

_____

_____

_____

_____

_____

3

Ruth's Decision
Ruth 1:14-22

On February 1, 2003, all around the world, people watched as seven astronauts prepared to return to earth on the space shuttle *Columbia*. With horror they saw the space shuttle disintegrate into millions of pieces when it re-entered the earth's atmosphere.

The tragedy was caused when a piece of insulating foam detached and hit the wing. No one imagined the disastrous consequences.

Like the piece of foam, it is sometimes the small, seemingly inconsequential decisions that can open the door to awful consequences in life. People do not plan to become alcoholics when they decide to take their first drink. People do not plan to die of cancer when they smoke their first cigarette. People do not expect to destroy their marriage with one tiny white lie. Poor decisions have a way of accumulating. That is why it's so important to make our decisions based on God's moral and individual will. When we do that, the consequences of those decisions will enhance our life rather than harm it.

Prayer

Praise you, Lord, for giving me rest, just as you promised. Not one word has failed of all your wonderful promises. You are my eternal God and my refuge. Your everlasting arms are under me and you drive my enemy out before me (1 Kings 8:56, page 266, and Deuteronomy 33:27, page 167).

Following Step by Step

There is nothing more important than following God's will. Inside His will we find joy, satisfaction, fulfillment, purpose, peace, surrender, sacrifice, putting others before ourselves—all of which are good. His will is not some hard-to-find, well-kept secret. He makes His will known to us in different ways.

Read Isaiah 58:11 (page 563).

How does God guide us?

What will He give us?

He wants us to be a *"well-watered, ever-flowing spring"*! Have you ever been around a spring? It is teeming with life. Southeastern Oregon has some barren, desolate land, but it is a beautiful place to drive through when hidden springs water the mountain areas and turn them a lush green. Wildflowers grow in abundance, and wildlife comes there to feed.

That's the beauty of being in God's will—not only are we teeming with life, but that life and energy spreads out to those around us. As believers, we do not have to fumble our way through life. God has a perfect plan for each of us. But how do we find what that plan is?

We learned last time that we discover how to make right decisions by knowing and obeying what God's Word teaches.

Read Proverbs 3:5-6 (page 482).

What are the three things it tells us to do in order to stay on the right path?

The middle instruction is key—"*do not depend on your own understanding*." That can be the hardest thing in the world to do sometimes. But our understanding of a situation can be faulty. God's understanding never is because He is omniscient. He sees where our decisions will take us in the future.

Trusting Him is a bit like using a GPS device to find your way to a destination. You're only given one step at a time. God rarely lays out the whole plan for us. He takes us one step at a time. A vivid example of His leading one step at a time is seen in how He guided the Israelites to the Promised Land. Read Exodus 13:21 (page 54).

Never once did God fail to make the pillar of cloud or pillar of fire visible to them. It was easy to see at all times. It stayed right in front of them. We do not have a pillar of cloud or fire today as they did. But as obedient followers of Christ we can experience God's guidance and have assurance of His leading through the study of His Word, prayer, the counsel of godly people, circumstances, and the work of the Holy Spirit in our lives.

Making Decisions Without Regrets

Naomi had let her close communication with God deteriorate to the point where she could only hear her own advice, and it kept leading her in the wrong direction. If you recall, when we saw her last, she had told her two daughters-in-law to return to their own families and their own gods.

It is a heartbreaking scene—the three women who have lost everything standing in the middle of a lonely road, clinging to each other and weeping. For around ten years they've lived together, celebrated together, laughed together, mourned together—and faced widowhood together. The thought of separating from Naomi is clearly devastating, as we see the young women begging to stay with her. But Naomi's mind is made up. She will return to Bethlehem alone. Read Ruth 1:14-18 (page 208). What did each woman decide to do?

Step into the drama that unfolds in these verses. Can you feel the terrible sorrow of these women? Imagine the pain when Orpah pulled away from their embrace, picked up her pack, and turned away from them. As she began retracing the steps toward Moab, did Naomi have second thoughts? Was she tempted to call after her? Did Orpah hurry away or walk slowly, expecting her sister-in-law to join her?

Again, there is no way to know. Her story brings to mind the words of John Greenleaf Whittier, American poet and abolitionist, who wrote, "For of all sad words of tongue or pen, the saddest are these: 'It might have been!'"

There are no "what might have been" situations when we follow in God's footsteps. There are no reasons for regret. Regret comes when we leave His footprints and make prints of our own. Orpah's story is like so many people who almost decide to follow God but aren't willing to fully commit their lives to Him. We each have the freedom to accept or reject His love, and just as Orpah's decision determined her future, so our decisions determine ours.

Both Orpah and Ruth loved their mother-in-law, but they expressed their love in different ways. Orpah kissed Naomi in affection. Ruth clung to Naomi in commitment. Look again at Ruth's statement of commitment to her mother-in-law in verses 16-17. Which of her promises to Naomi stands out to you most? Why?

Have you ever felt that level of commitment to someone or something? How did it affect your decisions?

In Ruth's decision, we see her sold-out commitment to embrace an entirely different life regardless of the cost. We will also see the immeasurable blessing that began to define her life from the point of decision on. Her story is a magnificent example of the result of full commitment to God. The moment we decide to exchange our way of life for His way, and fully embrace that commitment, we will begin to experience similar blessings. His rich promises will begin to bear fruit all around us.

That level of commitment comes with a cost. In every aspect, Ruth turned from her old way of life to her new way of life. She gave up her family, her friends, her belongings—even her *belief system!*

Can you think of a difficult choice you had to make that involved letting go of things you valued?

When you look back on that decision, how do you feel about it?

When thinking in terms of following God's will, what are some struggles you deal with in coming to a point where you are willing to exchange your will for His?

Have you ever wanted something so badly that you went against what you knew was God's will in order to satisfy your own will? What was the result?

Here is an unchanging truth: The closer we walk with God, the more our will matches His. The greater the distance between us, the greater the conflict between our two wills. If you are tired of being pulled in opposite directions, close the gap between you and God.

God Knows Best

His will for our lives is based in two things:

1. *He created us.* He knows us better than anyone else does. He knows us better than we know ourselves. He knows what excites us, dismays us, fulfills us, and inspires us. He knows our strengths and weaknesses, our capabilities and talents. He knows where we'll flourish and where we'll flounder. God knows it all, and in that knowledge, He created a unique plan that takes all of these things into account.

2. *He knows the future.* God knows what's going to happen the next minute, the next day, the next year, and the next decade—so He knows how to direct us.

Taking these two things into account, who is in a better position to know the right path for you to take—you or God?

The choices we make give us the opportunity to obey Him by choosing His way. When we do what He wants us to do, we are reaffirming our love for Him. And like Ruth, when we choose to follow

Him, we open our lives to the full expression of His love for us. Read
the following verses:

John 14:21-24 (page 823)

John 15:10 (page 824)

What is the one thing both of these passages said?

Love and obedience walk hand in hand, don't they? If we love God,
we will follow Him—we will trust His leading and not our own.

Now read Luke 6:46-49 (page 787).

God's will is filled with purpose and fulfillment. Any other direction will always fall short. It's just that simple. When we ignore His
will—or worse, when we manipulate His will to conform to ours—
the result will always disappoint us. Ruth chose God's will. She made
a complete break with the past. Her commitment was total and she
said it would last until her death!

Is there an area of your life that you have not fully relinquished to God? Is there something in your past that you
need to release, once and for all? Take some time right now
to reflect, then write down your thoughts.

If you're ready, tell God. Ask Him to help you fully let go.

The Fruit of Our Choices

Every decision we make has ongoing repercussions, not only for us but for the people around us. That's why it is so important to let God lead us in our decision making. Ruth made a wise decision that set the pattern for her life. She let no difficulties dissuade her, and ultimately she experienced benefits.

Eventually, Ruth and Naomi made it back to Bethlehem. Read Ruth 1:19 (page 208). How did the people respond to Naomi and Ruth's arrival?

The *"entire town"* was excited to see them! It sounds like a welcome-home party, doesn't it? According to Ruth 1:20-21, how did Naomi respond to their welcome?

Let's step into this scene for a moment and imagine together what it might have been like. Two women are seen approaching town, and it draws some attention. Two women traveling alone is not a common sight. Curiosity spreads, and soon everyone is gathered near the town's entrance to see who the two women are. As they draw closer, someone gasps, "Oh my goodness! That looks like Naomi! Could it possibly be?"

As Ruth and Naomi get closer, all the townspeople rush to meet them, crowding around to hug Naomi and welcome her back.

"Don't call me Naomi," she says to them. *"Instead call me Mara, for the Almighty has made life very bitter for me!"*

Has a wrong view of God affected your outlook, as it did Naomi's?

Ruth determined to look out for the needs of her mother-in-law. She knew what the right thing to do was and set her mind to do it, whatever the cost to her personally.

The right thing to do in every circumstance—no matter how devastating or painful—is to bring God glory through our response.

Read John 15:8 (page 824).

Bringing glory to God is simply focusing our life, attitude, and choices to be God-centered. We bring glory to Him through how we live and respond to life's circumstances and the people around us. Through prayer, godly living, loving and serving others, and repentance—we bring glory to Him. Imagine that! Our confession of the sin in our lives brings glory to Him. He is our Redeemer, and through confession of our sin, through our weakness, He is made strong and that brings glory to Him. We put the attention on Him as our primary focus and motivation for all we do. He gets the glory. He gets the attention through our lives.

Ruth's decision to stay with Naomi immediately began to bear fruit and, yes, bring God glory, just as our God-centered responses to adverse circumstances do. The wonderful thing to know is that we aren't on our own in finding the strength to keep doing the next right thing. God Himself will empower us. Read the following passages:

2 Peter 1:3-8 (page 938)

Philippians 2:12-15 (page 900)

What do verse 3 of the first passage and verse 13 of the second passage tell us?

Amazing, isn't it? God gives us all we need to live a godly life, including the *desire* to do so!

What does the first passage say He has given to help us make the right choices (verse 4)?

What is one of God's promises that you find most helpful in living your life in a way that glorifies Him?

Second Peter 1:5-7 (page 938) shows an interesting connection between various behaviors. How are we to supplement our faith?

How is moral excellence related to having a strong faith? The more our behavior is modified by God, the stronger our faith becomes, because we are more attuned to Him. And follow the list on down. The more knowledge we have of Him, the more willing we are to develop moral excellence, which results in self-control...and on and on, with the end result being that we are able to feel love toward everyone.

It is interesting to look at Naomi and Ruth, both of whom had suffered great tragedy. Naomi's response was to turn inward, hunching her shoulders around her pain, holding it tight and close. Ruth's response was to reach outward, toward Naomi.

The most effective balm for your own pain is to help someone else who is hurting. Have you ever experienced this personally? Please explain.

This next week, look for someone who could use a little loving attention. Ask God to use you to comfort them. Write the results of your actions below, so we can share them together next time.

───────── *Personal Reflection and Application* ─────────

From this chapter,

I see…

I believe…

I will…

────────────── ❧ ──────────────

Prayer

    God, I know that you began a good work within me, and you will continue your work until it is finally finished on the day when Christ Jesus returns. Don't let me get tired of doing what is good, because I know that at the right time I will reap a harvest of blessing if I don't give up (Philippians 1:6, page 899, and Galatians 6:9, page 894).

───────── *Thoughts, Notes, and Prayer Requests* ─────────

───────────────────────────────

───────────────────────────────

───────────────────────────────

───────────────────────────────

───────────────────────────────

───────────────────────────────

4

Israel's Custom
Ruth 2:1-16

My siblings and I sat around the kitchen table playing a game of Old Maid. It was our mother's birthday, but there'd been no happy celebration like before our father's death. Then there'd been lots of gifts and dinner out. Now it was just soup and our pitiful homemade gifts. Worst of all, Mom wasn't even home. She had night school.

A knock on the door sent the three of us running to see who it might be. My brother opened the door as my sister and I peeked out from behind him. It was a man from our church. "Is your mom home?" he asked. We shook our heads in silent unison. "Well, maybe you could hold the door open for me," he suggested. "I have some things to bring in."

We watched in growing awe as he carried in bag after bag of groceries. Soon the table, the kitchen counter, and even the floor were covered with bulging bags. As he set the last bag down and turned to leave he said, "Tell your mom the church says happy birthday!"

Although the bags were meant for her, we tore into them, holding up treasures such as Nestle's Instant Cocoa and Kraft Macaroni and Cheese—exotic, name-brand items we'd never had. We were so excited we decided to try our hand at baking a cake. While my brother read the recipe, I measured out the ingredients, and my little sister mixed them altogether. When the cake finished baking, we frosted it with a recipe of our own concoction that included a lot of blue food coloring. To complete the masterpiece we stuck red candles all over the top and sides, giving it the intriguing look of a wild blue porcupine.

What a celebration we had when my mother returned from class—the best party ever—as we celebrated not just her birthday, but the God who'd supplied all our needs, just as He promised!

Prayer

Thank you, Lord, that your eyes search the whole earth in order to strengthen those whose hearts are fully committed to you. You are a shield around me; you are my glory, the one who holds my head high (2 Chronicles 16:9a, page 343, and Psalm 3:3, page 415).

God Is Behind the Story

One of the reasons the book of Ruth is so fascinating is because it tells us a story—a great story—with lots of twists, turns, and surprises. It's fun to peek into someone's life and see how their life philosophies were formed and observe how the choices led to certain outcomes. It's one of the reasons biographies or autobiographies are so often bestsellers.

If you were to write your own autobiography, what is one of the clearest pieces of evidence you would include to show how God has worked in your life?

God created us so that we can receive His thoughts, return His love, and respond to His will. He also created us with a free will that allows us to accept or reject His thoughts, His love, and His guidance. Any time we choose to reject these things it is sin, and everyone who has ever lived is a sinner. Read Romans 3:23 (page 859).

Our sin nature means that we do not naturally want to love and obey God. When we decide to do His will, the first thing we must do is acknowledge our sin and receive His gift of forgiveness. Read Acts 3:19 (page 832).

When we receive His gift of forgiveness and the new life He wants to give us, our desires begin to change. Read Philippians 2:13 (page 900).

God's desire from the beginning of time has been to have a loving, willing relationship with us. He goes to huge lengths to make such a relationship desirable. When we come to the place where we are ready to exchange our old way of life for His new way of life, we enter into a whole new realm of possibilities never before imagined. Ruth's story is just one example of this.

Ruth's Decisions in Her New Home

Another reason the book of Ruth is so fascinating is that it gives us a vivid glimpse into the culture and customs of that time. This chapter gives us one of those glimpses. Read Ruth 2:1-3 (page 208).

What three words were used to describe Boaz in verse 1?

When Boaz enters the scene, you immediately suspect where the storyline is going. However, this isn't just another good story. This is a *true* story showcasing the providence of God.

What does Ruth decide to do in verse 2?

Ruth quickly realized she needed to find a way to provide for herself and her mother-in-law, and gleaning was the only option available to her—which brings us to one of the customs of that time.

Read the following passages and note what they say:

Deuteronomy 24:19-20 (page 157)

Leviticus 19:9-10 (page 94)

Gleaning was the welfare system that God established. It was how the poor, foreigners, widows, and orphans were provided for. During harvest, the hired men worked the field first. They would grasp handfuls of grain stalks, cut them off with a sickle, and lay them on the ground. Female workers came behind the men, gathering up and binding the stalks into bundles that would then be carted off to the threshing floor. The last group to enter the field was the gleaners, who were allowed to gather what the first two groups had left behind.

Gleaning was not an easy task, and women gleaners were especially vulnerable, often being victimized by the harvesters. And you can imagine the competition among the gleaners was fierce. These were desperate, hungry people, scrounging for their very lives. Depending on the growing conditions and the attitudes in the field, a gleaner could easily work all day and still go home hungry.[4]

When Ruth set out that morning to glean, she faced a long day of backbreaking work and potential peril. She didn't know what awaited her. She only knew that she and Naomi had to have something to eat.

Tucked into the middle of verse 3 is the kind of phrase you find in fairy tales—only this is no fairy tale. "*As it happened,*" it says, "*she found herself working in a field that belonged to Boaz.*" When we open our lives to the power of God, "*as it happened*" becomes a common occurrence because He is always working behind the scenes to our advantage.

Notice that God did not arrange for a flashing arrow to direct Ruth to Boaz's field. He didn't speak to her in an audible voice or give her a vision in the night. Ruth simply made the right decision to provide for her mother-in-law, and God guided her feet in the right direction. On a daily basis, as we do what we know is right, He guides us to where we need to be for our greatest benefit and more importantly, His good. Most of the time we're not even aware of it happening. It is only as we look back that we see His handprint on our life.

Can you look back on a time in your life when you can see this was the case?

Ruth had made a number of right decisions that led up to this life-changing encounter.

- She chose to believe in the living God instead of the false gods of her people.

- She chose to follow and care for her sad mother-in-law.

- She chose to support Naomi and herself by the humbling work of gleaning.

- She did not sit around waiting for the Lord to reveal His will. As she started to do something, God led her.

Each day Ruth kept doing the next right thing, putting Naomi's needs ahead of her own pride, trusting God to guide her steps. And He did—right into an *"as it happened"* circumstance that would change her life forever.

Clarifying What God Wants

Read the following verses. How can we know God's will according to each passage?

Psalm 119:105 (page 470)

James 1:5 (page 930)

Ephesians 5:15-17 (pages 897-898)

James 1:21-22 (page 930)

Psalm 37:3-5 (page 429)

Isaiah 30:21 (pages 539-540)

All of these directives work together to clarify God's will in our lives. There is no secret about finding His will. We find it as we behave the way He wants us to behave, always doing the right thing. As we follow His steps, He will continually be leading us in the direction we should go.

The more we confidently trust God and apply His Word to our lives, the more we will be aware of what He is saying to us through circumstances, people, His Word, and the Holy Spirit—and the more we will find living in His will to be a natural lifestyle.

> "The will of God consists...of a life lived for God right where we are. It is not a set of ideal circumstances we imagine for ourselves. It is the godly course we set for our lives in the circumstances we face."
>
> —Jerry Sittser

The Bible makes it very clear what not to trust when seeking God's will. What do the following verses say we should avoid when living a lifestyle in God's will?

Zechariah 10:2 (page 724)

Micah 5:12 (page 706)

Galatians 5:19-21 (page 893)

God and His Word are trustworthy sources for making decisions. He will never lead us astray!

God's Plan Starts to Unfold

Read Ruth 2:4-7 (pages 208-209).

Did you notice how Boaz greeted his workers? It gives us insight into his character. So now we know that not only is he wealthy and influential, he's also a godly man. And he's observant! Right away he spots Ruth and asks the foreman about her. Within the foreman's answer, we gain further insight into Ruth's character when he tells Boaz she is a hard worker.

Read Ruth 2:8-10 (page 209).

What steps does Boaz take to help Ruth?

Do you see how God is guiding her steps? He is blessing her right actions, just as He always does! When have you clearly felt His blessing as a result of doing the right thing, even though it may not have been something you were eager to do?

God loves to bless His followers, and His blessings are never stingy. See how He continues to help Ruth in verses 11-16.

What further steps does Boaz take to watch out for Ruth?

Boaz exuded kindness in his attitude and actions toward Ruth and those around him. In the last chapter we were going to watch for someone we thought could use a little loving attention. Did you find someone?

How did they respond to your kindness?

Ruth is a sparkling example of how God guides our steps even when we are not aware of it. She is also an example of how, when we reach out to help someone else, our own life is enlarged. Keep your eyes open in the coming week for someone else who could benefit from a little loving attention.

"Kindness is more than deeds. It is an attitude, an expression, a look, a touch. It is anything that lifts another person."

—C. Neil Strait

Personal Reflection and Application

From this chapter,

I see...

I believe...

I will...

♾

Prayer

Lord, you are my Redeemer. You are the Lord my God, who teaches me what is good for me and leads me along the paths I should follow (Isaiah 48:17, page 555).

Thoughts, Notes, and Prayer Requests

_____

_____

_____

_____

_____

_____

_____

5

A New Beginning
Ruth 2:17-23

Sarah had lived a long and fruitful life, following God faithfully. She'd outlived her husband and most of her family and friends. Now in her eighties, with her health failing, she faced one final decision—where to finish out her days. She knew she could no longer stay in her beloved home, and that saddened her. Although she'd lived frugally all her life, the lovely care facility nearby was far beyond her means. Her only option was the county nursing home, a place she dreaded to call home.

A young woman came to visit her one day, a new Christian, full of optimism and a strong belief in God's promises. "Sarah, you don't have to worry," the young woman told her after hearing her story. "You have always been faithful to God and He will take care of you now. He won't forsake you."

Sarah smiled at the young woman's words, warmed by them even though she knew where she'd be moving. As she made preparations for her move to the nursing home, she called the local auction house to help with the sale of her furniture. She was surprised to learn that her old, outdated furniture was actually quite valuable. Then, a trip to the bank to close out her safe deposit box revealed it to be full of even more valuable war bonds her husband had purchased years ago.

She'd forgotten all about them. When all of Sarah's possessions were tallied up, it turned out she had more than enough for a small apartment in the nearby care facility. The young woman had been right. Sarah needn't have worried. God keeps His promises.

❧

Prayer

I praise you, Lord—my God, my Savior! For each day you carry me in your arms. I wait quietly before you, for my victory comes from you. You alone are my rock and my salvation, my fortress where I will never be shaken (Psalm 68:19, page 443, and Psalm 62:1, page 440).

Following in God's Footsteps

So far in this study, we've learned that God's will isn't some deep, hard-to-discern secret. We find it as we become familiar with the Bible, as we pray, and as we commit to follow in His footsteps. But what exactly does it mean to follow in His footsteps? Read the following verses:

Philippians 2:2-8 (page 900)
Romans 12:10 (page 866)

What do you see as the key thought in these verses?

It sounds simple, doesn't it—to put others' needs ahead of our own—but oh, it is so hard to actually practice. If we make that our goal, everything else will fall into place, for that is the mind of Christ. He, who had every right in the world to do whatever He wanted in the world, never once put His needs before ours. We always held first place in His mind. It is overwhelming to contemplate, isn't it? Take a moment and reflect on the scope of God's love for you. Feel free to write your thoughts down.

Ruth fully relinquished her own need for physical and emotional comfort in order to address Naomi's needs and show her love. She looked beyond Naomi's bitterness and saw her grief and pain. That gave her the motivation to set her own needs aside to address Naomi's. She made the decision to save her mother-in-law regardless of what she had to endure and, just as promised, God empowered her every step of the way. What do the following verses also show us about following in His footsteps?

1 Thessalonians 4:1-8 (page 906)

Hebrews 13:16 (page 929)

As Ruth followed in God's footsteps, He guided her right to the field she needed to be in, to meet the man she needed to meet. It was no accident that she found her way into the field owned by Boaz, and now her story is about to take a dramatic change.

As exhausted as Ruth must have been at the end of her long day of gleaning, excitement from all that had happened surely must have propelled her home in record time.

Read Ruth 2:17-19 (page 209).

Often gleaners obtained only enough grain to keep starvation at bay. But, thanks to Boaz, after only one day of gleaning Ruth carried home about 25 pounds of barley—the equivalent of two weeks' wages! Oh, how quickly God can change the picture when we faithfully follow Him!

For ten years, Naomi had been walking in one form or another of hopelessness. The hopelessness of widowhood, the hopelessness of two marriage unions that were explicitly against God's will, the hopelessness of no grandchildren, the hopelessness of both her sons' death, and the hopelessness of a future in which she had no one to protect or provide for her. But then her daughter-in-law, Ruth, grabs hold of the true and sovereign God. She matches her steps to His and determines to keep doing the next right thing, no matter how difficult, humiliating, or fearful. An attitude such as Ruth's cannot help but bring about blessings, such as the ones that occurred that day as she gleaned in the field owned by Boaz.

Naomi's Turnaround

Can't you imagine the scene when Ruth got home that night and dramatically displayed all her grain? Can you see Naomi running her fingers through the grain in delighted wonder as she asks Ruth where she got it all? Don't you figure that their words tumbled over each other in their excitement? What an evening of celebration they must have had together. And it appears this good news finally broke through the terrible wall of doubt Naomi allowed herself to construct between her and God.

A delightful picture of God's abundance is found in verse 18. What did Ruth do with the barley from her meal?

God is detail-oriented. He leaves nothing out. What a subtle yet unmistakable reminder to Naomi that her accusation of His abandonment was incorrect. He is not a God of bitterness; He is a God of love and mercy. When Ruth left to go glean that morning, Naomi was a grieving, bitter woman whose life was running on empty. But evening produced a complete turnaround in her outlook.

Notice the shift in Naomi's attitude from Ruth 1:13,20-21 to Ruth 2:20.

Do you see how she moves from feelings of rejection and bitterness to feelings of gratitude in response to Boaz's treatment of Ruth? What a difference a day makes!

Can you think of a turnaround day in your own life? What was going on at the time, and what caused the turnaround?

One reason for Naomi's sudden turnaround in attitude is that she realized Boaz could be the means by which she might regain some of what had been lost by going to Moab. What did Naomi say about him in the last part of verse 20?

To see what she meant, read Leviticus 25:23-25 (page 100).

Boaz was the reason for Naomi's new hope. He could buy back her land for her, and she would no longer be destitute. This verse gives us another intriguing glimpse into the culture of that time. God had given Israel the land of Canaan for their permanent possession. Each tribe had received a certain section of the land, which in turn was divided among all the families of that tribe. This was God's heritage given to each family and they were never to leave their land. If they had a crop failure (which God said He would send if the people were unfaithful to Him), they could sell the land to someone else until the fiftieth year.

Every 50 years of Israel's history came a year called the Year of Jubilee. Read Leviticus 25:8-17 (page 100). Jot down the information you find most interesting.

How do you think this would go over in today's culture?

Leviticus 25:14 and 17 repeat a phrase, stressing the importance of what God is saying to the Israelites. What is the phrase?

That selfless attitude that focused on fairness rather than making a profit honored God. His laws were designed to keep the land He had given to the Israelites within their families, even if some of the people fell on hard times. It was the way God provided for the care of the poor and for the general economy of the country. During the Year of Jubilee, all debts were canceled.

Naomi's sudden change of attitude is very often similar to ours when we are living through difficult times. It's easy to feel like God has turned His back on us when things go against us. Then, when our circumstances improve, we feel like He is finally coming to our rescue. The truth is, He never leaves us—we leave Him! God didn't leave Naomi when the famine came to her land, or when her husband and sons died. He longed to help her through those times but her attitude made her blind to Him.

However, even in her acute distress and sorrow, He stood nearby, waiting for her to turn back to Him. And all the while, He was working behind the scenes. It was no accident that Ruth became Naomi's daughter-in-law. God even worked through Naomi's poor decisions and express disobedience to bring about His ultimate good plan for her. And now, as her heart begins to once again open toward Him, we'll see the plan come into fruition.

The invaluable lesson to be learned from Naomi's story is that the years of hardship and stress she endured were not of God's making. They were the result of the long series of unwise decisions Naomi (and Elimelech) made that left God out of the equation.

Has there been a time when you've done the same thing? What was the result?

Hope Comes from God

When Boaz enters the scene, he provides a beautiful picture of what Jesus does for us. We may feel discouraged and bitter. Our future may look hopeless. But when we open our heart to Jesus, our situation changes! He turns heartache to joy. Ruth is a picture of an unbeliever who comes to Christ by faith. It doesn't matter what is in our past, Jesus sees only our faith in Him and welcomes us with open arms.

Boaz did for Naomi and Ruth what God does for us. He provided for their needs. Read the following verses. What does God promise to do in each passage?

1 Peter 5:6-7 (page 937)

Matthew 6:25-32 (pages 737-738)

Philippians 4:19 (page 901)

2 Corinthians 9:8 (page 886)

These verses show that God provides not just for our physical needs but our emotional needs as well. There is no doubt that He led Ruth's footsteps to Boaz's field.

How does God lead our footsteps today?

What is a physical need He has provided for you recently?

What is an emotional need He has provided for you recently?

Read the following verses and note what they say.

Proverbs 16:9 (page 492)

Isaiah 48:17 (page 555)

Psalm 32:8 (page 427)

Isaiah 58:11 (page 563)

John 16:13 (page 824)

Psalm 37:23 (page 430)

What is the common theme among all these verses?

What did the last verse tell us about God's attitude toward us?

Does it amaze you to realize that God delights in the details of your life? I think of my little granddaughter, in whom I delight. I delight in her smiles and even her tears, marveling at how they spill from her eyes. I delight in her physical and mental growth. I delight in her personality. I even delight in her eyelashes! And it astounds me to realize that God delights in each one of us in a much greater way.

Know this—even if *you* don't feel delight-worthy, God finds you delightful. Take a few moments and imagine His delight in you. What do you think He would notice?

Now let's read the final three verses of the second chapter—Ruth 2:21-23 (page 209).

Ruth obviously had a strong work ethic. In her desire to care for herself and her mother-in-law she worked straight through two harvest seasons.

How do you think it must have felt to finally have more than enough food, and to know they might be able to get their land back?

Hope is a powerful motivator and sustainer. It is essential to the quality of one's life. Once Naomi caught a glimmer of hope, she was finally able to crack through the wall of darkness she'd constructed around herself. Is there a circumstance in your life that appears hopeless? Is there a prayer that God seems to be ignoring? Don't let your attitude toward it build a wall between you and Him. Take some time right now and tell Him how you're feeling about this matter. Ask Him to renew your trust in His ability to work through the circumstance in a way that will be best for all involved.

Personal Reflection and Application

From this chapter,

I see...

I believe...

I will...

Prayer

Lord, I will not throw away my confident trust in you. I will remember the great reward it brings me! I know that patient endurance is what I need now, so that I will continue to do your will. Then I will receive all that you have promised (Hebrews 10:35-36, page 926).

Thoughts, Notes, and Prayer Requests

6

Ruth's Request
Ruth 3:1-18

I t was not how she'd expected to spend the next six-and-a-half years of her life. She had two teenagers to finish raising and an ailing father who needed her care. She was also in an intense political battle to become the next president of the nation of Colombia. Against the advice of those near her, she decided to keep a commitment to give a speech in an area where antigovernment terrorists were known to be active. The day of the speech, she kissed her father goodbye, not knowing she'd never see him again. He would die while she was being held hostage deep in the Colombian jungles.

In her book *Even Silence Has an End*, Ingrid Betancourt wrote of her experience:

> *When you're chained by the neck to a tree, and deprived of all freedom—the freedom to move around, to talk, to eat, to drink, to carry out your most basic bodily needs—well, it took me several years to realize it, but you still have the most important freedom of all, which no one can take away from you: that is the freedom to choose what kind of person you want to be.*[5]

✑

Prayer

Thank you, Lord, for leaving me with the gift of peace of mind and heart. I know that your peace is a gift the world cannot give. So I will not be troubled or afraid. I will be strong and courageous, and will put my hope in you (John 14:27, page 824, and Psalm 31:24, page 427).

When Naomi told her daughters-in-law to return to their own land, one of the reasons she gave was that she had no other sons for them to marry. Having a man's name carried on was so important that God gave laws about it. Read Deuteronomy 25:5-6 (page 158).

Aren't you glad to be living now rather than then?

In the case of Naomi's family, it meant that Elimelech's brother, or closest relative, was to marry his widow, Naomi. Both Elimelech's sons were dead and there were no sons to carry on the family inheritance. When Boaz enters the picture, a plan begins to form in Naomi's mind, a plan that will secure her daughter-in-law's future. Now that she has broken out of her paralyzing depression, her focus has moved from herself to Ruth. Read Ruth 3:1 (page 209).

If Ruth were still single when Naomi died, she would be among the most vulnerable of society. An alien and a widow—easy prey for anyone who wanted to take advantage of her or harm her. According to the law, Elimelech's closest relative would marry Naomi. While this would restore Elimelech's land to her, it was too late for her to have another child to carry on her deceased husband's name. However, if Boaz married *Ruth*, Elimelech's land would still be restored and Ruth's future would be secure. It was the best possible solution for all involved, but there were obstacles between her plan and its fruition.

First of all, it was men who carried out all marriage negotiations, but there was no man to speak for either Naomi or Ruth. Secondly, in regard to marriage, Ruth had nothing in her favor, and she had plenty against her. She was an alien, she was known to be barren, she had no dowry—in short, she had nothing at all to bring to the table from that culture's perspective. Thus Naomi is forced to be creative. And, as we'll soon see, creativity is her forte.

Naomi's Plan

Read Ruth 3:2-7 (page 209).

> Oh my! The minute you came to the word *"perfume,"* could you tell where this story was going? According to verse 5, what was Ruth's response to Naomi's plan?

Did you sense any hesitation? Do you think, perhaps, she had a sense that God was unfolding before her eyes His greater plan for her and those around her?

When we walk in God's will, we are following His leading and His prompting. We trust that He brings all things together for His good purpose. Sometimes He brings it about on His own, and sometimes, such as in this moment with Ruth, He requires our courage and our trust in His leading. Regardless of how uncertain the path may seem, or how treacherous and hard, a life of following God's will is the best for us, just as Ruth is about to find out.

Naomi's specific instructions show her concern for both Boaz's and Ruth's feelings and reputation, in light of the bold plan she was implementing. She told Ruth to wait until nightfall, after the feasting was over and all of the workers had gone home. That way Boaz would be alone, giving them both privacy and darkness to alleviate embarrassment should he choose not to pursue the role of family redeemer.

What do you think Ruth's thoughts were as she went to the river to bathe and as she dabbed herself with perfume? What emotions would she have been grappling with as she took off her drab widow's dress for the first time since her husband's death and put on her very best? That act alone would have been fraught with symbolism and emotion as she removed the constant reminder of all she had lost and then put on nice clothing. How long had it been since she'd felt beautiful? As she brushed her hair until it gleamed, do you think she pondered the steps she would be taking that night—and all the previous steps that had led her to this moment?

Describe a time when you stood at such a symbolic crossroads in your life, looking back on your past and ahead toward your future.

Imagine the level of courage it took for Ruth to follow her mother-in-law's daring plan. So much was at stake! Do you think her heart pounded as she slipped through the darkness to the threshing floor? As she stayed hidden from view, waiting for Boaz to fall asleep, did her palms grow sweaty and her breath short?

Imagine her tiptoeing over to where he lay sleeping, trying to discern in the darkness which end was his head and which was his feet. Did her clothing rustle against the stone floor as she eased herself down by his feet? Did she eventually fall asleep—or did she lay there, frozen, waiting for Boaz to awaken and find her?

Read verses 8 and 9.

When Boaz does awake and finds Ruth at his feet, he knows what she wants even without her saying a word. He can see that her widow's garments are gone; he can smell her sweet perfume. Daniel Block, in his commentary on Ruth, points out the ways Naomi's plan gives new meaning to *irregular* according to the customs of those times. You

have "a foreigner propositioning an Israelite; a woman propositioning a man; a young person propositioning an older person; a destitute field worker propositioning the landowner."[6] It's a beyond crazy
situation.

There are many unknown elements at this juncture of the story,
and biblical scholars have different ideas of what took place that night
between Ruth and Boaz. The truth is, we simply do not know exactly
what happened. It's not even certain what meaning was attached to
the actions that *did* occur. One aspect everyone agrees on, however, is
that Naomi's intentions were pure.

Carolyn Custis James says that Naomi's "whole purpose is to
secure Ruth's safety, not to jeopardize her future. She has taken the
greatest care to avoid tarnishing Ruth's reputation and is sending her
to a man she has every reason to believe will not exploit the situation
to his own advantage but will receive her daughter-in-law with respect
and honor."[7]

The Redeemer Responds

Boaz's response to Ruth when he finds her at his feet is further proof that the actions she undertook that night in no way
crossed the line. He clearly did not feel she had dishonored him
or was trying to force him into marriage. In fact, just the opposite is the case. What was his reply to her in verses 10 and 11?

Let's take a closer look at verse 11. What did Boaz say in the
first sentence?

"Don't worry about a thing." How do you think those words fell on Ruth's ears?

From the moment her husband had fallen ill and died, she'd had *everything* to worry about! There had never been a time since when she hadn't had something to worry about. And how extreme must her worry have been just in the last handful of hours as she'd carried out Naomi's daring instructions? Oh, how blessed those words must have been to her worry-worn psyche!

What does Boaz say he would do?

Can you remember someone saying something similar to you when you were really stressed? "No worries! I'll take care of it"? How did those words make you feel?

We can be sure that is exactly how Ruth was feeling—but probably multiplied many times over. Naomi's plan was surpassing her wildest expectations. But Boaz added one more thing in verse 11. What was it?

Do you realize what a remarkable compliment this was? The whole town held her in high regard in spite of the fact she was from the despised country of Moab.

People take note of honorable behavior. It has a way of tearing down social barriers and establishing respect. This is what other people should say about us as Christ-followers. Our behavior should always bring honor to God and make Him look good.

Do you have someone in your life who brings honor to God? How?

Before we continue, there's a little side trip we should take to a time a little further back in history. Not long before the period of time we're studying now, the Israelites planned an attack on the city of Jericho (Joshua 2, pages 168-169, and Joshua 6, page 171). In preparation, they sent two spies into the city to ascertain what they would be up against in the attack. The king of Jericho was told of their presence, and the two spies had to flee for their lives. They had been staying at an inn owned by a prostitute named Rahab. At the risk of her life, she hid them from the king's men and helped them escape over the city wall.

In return for her help, they promised that she, and all who were in her house, would not be harmed when Israel attacked Jericho. All she had to do was hang a scarlet rope from the window of her house so the Israelite soldiers would know to protect the inhabitants.

The Israelites conquered Jericho in short order, and as promised, Rahab and her family were saved. They were assimilated into the Israelite people. In another "as it turned out" situation, Rahab married Salmon, an Israelite, and they were blessed with a son. Guess what his name was?

Boaz!

Is it any wonder that Boaz was impressed with Ruth? He recognized a woman of courage and faith when he saw one—after all, he had been raised by one.

Redemption Begins

Okay, back to our original story, Naomi's carefully thought-out plan suddenly hits a big bump. According to Ruth 3:12, what is it?

Oops! This casts the two women's future right back into jeopardy—and things were looking so good there for a while. Have you ever had a plan that seemed to be coming together so smoothly, but suddenly started to unravel before your very eyes? How did you respond?

How do you reaffirm your trust in God's wisdom when a plan that you thought was from Him goes awry? If you're currently in a situation like this, take some time right now to pray and reflect on the situation.

It is comforting to know that while we cannot see the big picture, God can. As we keep our eyes fixed on Him and less fixed on the goals or destination, we can be assured that we are in His will. We shouldn't simply focus on specific outcomes or goals that we think should happen. Instead let's keep ourselves attentive to serving the Lord and living for Him right where we are. Following His leading is not based on our present comfort or circumstances. Following His leading is about following what we know He has told us to do—and He speaks to us in His Word!

Boaz immediately calmed Ruth's fears, however, in regard to the "bump." What was his backup plan if the nearest family redeemer refused Ruth?

He showed such assurance in his response that Ruth would be taken care of: *"As surely as the LORD lives!"* When Ruth returned home to Naomi she would have no reason to second-guess what had taken place that night. Regardless of what happened, Boaz had made it clear she would be taken care of.

Did you notice the word he used in regard to what he would do? *"I will redeem you myself!"* This is such an important element in the book of Ruth. We already talked some about the family redeemer (or kinsman-redeemer) in an earlier chapter. But let's look at it more closely now. Two things were paramount in ancient Israelite culture: maintaining the family name and maintaining the family land. This is why so much depended on Ruth's encounter with Boaz. Elimelech's land had already been lost, and with the death of both sons, neither of whom had children, his name would be lost too.

Because of the importance of land and names in that culture, laws were put in place to protect them. The levirate law protected the family name. It stated that a man would marry his brother's widow and that the first son born of that union would carry on the dead brother's name. The Mosaic Law stated that if a family member lost their land, the nearest relative—known as the family redeemer—would purchase the land to keep it in the family. These two laws required an extensive amount of time and loyalty in order to abide by them, and there often were circumstances when the redeemer would sacrifice his personal inheritance, along with his son's, in order to honor the law and the family. It became a case of "doing the right thing" regardless of the personal cost. When Boaz promised to redeem Ruth, he was assuring her that both Elimelech's name and land would be preserved, thus securing her own future. He made her a selfless promise and then followed through by keeping his word.

The word *redeem* is one of the most beautiful words in the English language. The *Merriam-Webster Dictionary* defines it in several ways: "to buy or win back," "to free from what distresses or harms," "to extricate from or help to overcome something detrimental," "to release from blame or debt" and, finally, "to free from the consequences of sin."

Boaz was promising all of these things to Ruth. He promised to win back her security, to free her from her distresses, to extricate her from her detrimental circumstances. But do you see the bigger picture we are looking at here? In the story of Ruth and Boaz, God gave us a picture of what He has done for us.

When Jesus came to earth and died for our sins, He became our family redeemer (kinsman-redeemer). When we acknowledge Jesus as the Son of God, who died for our sins, He redeems us. Although we are not always protected from harm while on earth (because we live in an imperfect world with imperfect people), we are assured that God never leaves us. He is with us through the fires of adversity. He is a very present help in trouble. He releases us from blame, guilt, and shame, and most wonderful of all, He frees us from the punishment of sin, which is eternal death. As Boaz was willing to become Ruth's redeemer, in much more magnified terms, Jesus became our Redeemer, who paid the price for our sins and proclaimed us *free*! We need to receive this gift and follow Him.

Read the following verses on Christ's redemption.
Romans 6:23 (page 861)
Romans 5:6-9 (page 860)
Romans 10:13 (page 864)

What does the last verse say we must do in order to be saved
from eternal death?

If you haven't made the decision to accept God's forgiveness of sin
through Christ's death on the cross, it is not too late—God is waiting
for you to respond to His gift of redemption. Take some time and talk
to God about it. (For more information, read the "Know God" section on pages 113–115 in the back of this study book.)

Now let's finish the chapter. Read Ruth 3:14-18 (page 210).

By telling her to stay the rest of the night, Boaz was protecting
Ruth's reputation. The grain he gave her to take back to Naomi was
further assurance to both women that they would be taken care of.

The third chapter ends on an uncertain note for everyone. Naomi
doesn't know if her plan will work. Boaz doesn't know if he will be
able to redeem Naomi's property and marry Ruth. Ruth doesn't know
if she will end up being passed off to a perfect stranger. For the time
being it's a waiting game for the two women until they hear back
from Boaz.

What is Naomi's advice to her daughter-in-law in verse 18?

Don't you hate those words? It's the last thing in the world you want to hear when you're waiting for something big. What are some things in your life that have been worth waiting for?

What did God teach or show you in the process of waiting?

In the next chapter, we're going to discover the value of Ruth's patience in waiting.

—————— *Personal Reflection and Application* ——————

From this chapter,

I see...

I believe...

I will...

Prayer

Father, you are so rich in kindness and grace that you purchased my freedom with the blood of your Son and forgave my sins. You have showered your kindness on me, along with all wisdom and understanding. I praise you for sending my Redeemer and mighty Savior (Ephesians 1:7-8, page 895, and Luke 1:68-69, page 780).

Thoughts, Notes, and Prayer Requests

7

The Result of Right Decisions
Ruth 4:1-22

It had been a long day of driving, and every muscle ached from lack of movement. After checking into our motel room, my friend and I drove to a nearby diner for a quick bite to eat. Our server was quite chatty and stopped by our table each time she passed. She was new to town and had a little boy she was raising alone; she was worried about making ends meet and being a good mom. We listened and encouraged her as best we could.

It was one of those meals where nothing was quite up to standard, but my friend and I decided to take the high road—our server had a difficult enough job as it was. We each left a generous tip, hoping it would bring a smile to her face after we left.

The next day we drove another 60 miles to a small community where I was speaking. As I got up to speak I noticed a young woman sitting at a center table. She looked familiar but I couldn't place her for the life of me. About halfway through my talk it hit me—it was our server from the night before!

So many thoughts buzzed through my mind that I could barely stay on script. What if we'd rebuffed her attempts to converse? What if we'd complained about our food and service? What if we'd left a chintzy tip? All the insignificant decisions we'd scarcely given thought to the night before were in my face today. Because we had made a series of right decisions, we could feel confident that God used our encounter with the server for good.

Afterward, I made a beeline for her table and she met me halfway. Turned out her grandmother had invited her to the luncheon, and she had come since it was her day off. Was it a divine appointment? Perhaps—but only because of the groundwork that was unknowingly laid the night before.

Prayer

God, thank you for the Scriptures, which are inspired by you and are useful to teach me what is true and to make me realize what is wrong in my life. Thank you for the way they correct me when I am wrong and teach me to do what is right (2 Timothy 3:16, page 915).

God's *Hesed* Way of Life

The book of Ruth has a fairy-tale quality to it—a too-good-to-be-true aspect. The fact that it is *not* a fairy tale makes the way Ruth loved her mother-in-law beyond remarkable. It makes Boaz's kindness and generosity hard to believe. The explanation for their attitudes can be found in a tiny Hebrew word that appears frequently in the Hebrew Scriptures. The word is *hesed,* and it is translated into English in a variety of ways: *kindness, mercy, loyalty, loving-kindness, steadfastness,* and *love*—to name a few. Most often it is translated as *kindness* or *loving-kindness.*

Hesed is the way God intends for us to live. It's the way Jesus lived while on earth—continually exhibiting this most important character quality. *Hesed* moves a person to reach out to others without consideration of how it will benefit him or her. It is utterly selfless in action and motivated by an attitude of extreme kindness.

The word *hesed* is used three times in Ruth. First, in Ruth 1:8, when Naomi tells her daughters-in-law to return home. She says *"May the* LORD *reward you for your kindness to your husbands and to me."* In Ruth 2:20, when Naomi hears of Boaz's graciousness, she says, *"He is showing his kindness to us as well as to your dead husband."* The third time *hesed* appears is Ruth 3:10, when Boaz says, *"You are showing even more family loyalty now than you did before."* Carolyn Custis James boils *hesed* down to this concept: "Someone cares and has freely made it their business to look out for you." It's what Ruth did for Naomi, what Boaz did for Ruth and Naomi—and most important of all, it's what Jesus does for us. He cares for us and has freely made it His business to look out for us.[8]

Redemption Is Achieved

We finished the previous chapter with the dismaying news that Boaz was not the first in line to be the family redeemer for Elimelech's property, nor to be a husband to Ruth to ensure the continuance of Elimelech's family name. Someone else was a closer relative. Read Ruth 4:1-3 (page 210).

In ancient days, the gate of a walled city, such as Bethlehem, was where business was conducted. Judges and elders sat at the gate to take care of their official duties. Everything was conducted in full view and in the hearing of any who wanted to listen. Since the gate was the city's gathering place, Boaz knew he would most likely find his relative there, and sure enough, he did. He gathers ten men together to witness the transaction and gets right down to business. Did you notice he didn't mention the matter of Ruth at the beginning? Why do you think he did this?

Before we get further into the business transaction, let's make sure we understand what is at stake for the man who redeems Elimelech's property. Whoever redeems the land will own it *unless* Naomi should have a son. In that case, the entire piece of land goes to the son. In other words, the man would pay for land but it would go to Naomi's son. However, since Naomi is too old to have a child, it looks like a very good deal for the family redeemer. Without the possibility of a son, acquiring the land will increase the family redeemer's wealth.

Read verse 4 and note what the man decides.

He claims his right as the family redeemer! He wants Naomi's land. This means Naomi and Ruth will be at the mercy of a man who is so unnoteworthy that history doesn't even bother to record his name! This doesn't bode well at all for the two women, does it?
But Boaz knows what he's doing. Read verse 5.

Don't you love it? Whatever is going on internally, Boaz remains calm. He casually throws in an "Oh, by the way…" which changes everything because Ruth was of childbearing age. Even though she had been childless up to this point, the man couldn't be sure she would stay that way. What is his response in verse 6?

And so the responsibility of being the family redeemer legally falls on Boaz's willing shoulders. He is willing to redeem Ruth even though she owns no dowry or property; she has nothing but the responsibility of an aging mother-in-law. He is willing to risk his own inheritance in order to secure Ruth's inheritance. And if God should choose to bless their union, he is willing to raise up a child to carry on another man's name. Boaz's behavior is the very definition of *hesed*.

Read Ruth 4:7-10 (page 210).

What was the custom in Israel for transferring a right of purchase?

What was the ultimate purpose in Boaz purchasing the land from Naomi?

No one ever loses respect for making a right decision. Boaz was a well-respected man in Bethlehem even before Ruth and Naomi entered his life. But his decision that day in the marketplace earned him even greater respect. What was the response of the witnesses in Ruth 4:11-12 (page 210)?

When they asked God to bless Boaz's union with Ruth, the examples they cited are of significance: Rachel and Leah, sisters whose 12 sons formed the 12 tribes of Israel; and Tamar, a woman who, like Naomi and Ruth, had to become extremely creative and bold in order to see that the name of her dead husband continued. Next time you read your Bible, you might enjoy reading her story in Genesis 38 (pages 32-33).

Reflecting the Heart of God

Boaz had no way of knowing what the future held for him the day he stood at the city gate proclaiming the onlookers as witnesses to the transaction he'd just made. His motives were inspired by a spirit of selflessness that came straight from the heart of God—and God never fails to reward such selflessness. And unbeknownst to him, as a result of this decision, a future king was now in the making. But even more remarkable than that, Boaz had just unwittingly knit himself into a divinely ordained holy lineage—the earthly lineage of Jesus Christ!

The decisions Boaz made were in line with God's will, because, as a result of his relationship with God, Boaz reflected His heart. The most important step in knowing God's will for your life is having a personal relationship with

> "The decisions we make turn around and make us."
>
> —Haddon Robinson

Him. It is the most important decision you'll ever make.

The small decisions we make are as important as the larger decisions, because each opens the door for another. Each helps to form our attitudes and responses. And each has the potential to lead us either closer or farther away from the will of God.

Problems begin when we make our own plans and then try to fit them into God's plan. Listen to your spirit when you are grappling with a decision. Is it struggling against God the Holy Spirit? Do you feel anxious or unsettled? That's a huge red flag. The Holy Spirit brings a sense of peace, not anxiety. If you find yourself rationalizing a decision, that is another red flag. Doing the right thing never needs to be rationalized.

God is not going to force us to go against our own will—but He will work within us to lead us in the best direction for our own well-being. The more familiar and responsive we become with the Spirit's nudging, the more likely we are to move in the right direction.

Following in God's will does not mean we will never experience heartache, tragedy, or even failure. Life is unpredictable. We make mistakes. We are surrounded by others who make mistakes, and their lives bump into ours. But being in God's will means, like Boaz, our heart will be in sync with His. Our actions and reactions will be based in an attitude of *hesed*—a desire to make life better for those He brings into our pathway.

Ruth and Naomi both suffered terrible sorrow and huge life setbacks. As Ruth sorrowed, she set herself aside to help Naomi, and God guided her to Boaz.

Do you remember the difficulties in the beginning of this story? It started with famine and death. But God never stopped working through these tragic events. He was putting the right people in the right place at the right time. He was not limited by Elimelech's lack of faith. He used Elimelech's decision to move his family to Moab to build faith in Ruth and bring her to Bethlehem.

How have you seen God working behind the scenes in your life?

The Blessing of the Choice to Follow God

As we've already discussed, we can discern God's will in a number of ways. Spending significant time in the Bible is one of the most important ways. Prayer is essential to knowing God's will. Paying attention to the internal nudges of the Holy Spirit is another way, along with seeking the counsel of godly people. What are some other ways we can know His will?

The key to all of these ways is asking yourself if they are in agreement. The Holy Spirit will *never* prompt you to do something that does not agree with what the Bible says. If you feel like you should do one thing but the Bible says differently, then—it is not the Holy Spirit leading you. Naomi and Elimelech felt like they should go to Moab to ride out the famine, but that feeling was in direct opposition to God's instruction in the Old Testament. It is very easy to be misled by our feelings. That's why consistent time in Bible study and prayer is absolutely essential in knowing God's will.

"There's no need for you to be burdened by or gripped with a paralyzing fear that you are not in God's will. If you are seeking Him and being obedient to what He has placed before you today, then *you are* in His purposes for now, and that is all He is asking of you and me."

—Priscilla Shirer

Some decisions don't require discernment—they just require obedience to God's moral law as we talked about in the first chapter. In Boaz's day, the law stated that the next closest relative should be the family redeemer. Boaz didn't have to pray to discern God's will in that matter—he just did it because it was the right thing to do.

God's moral laws are clear, giving us definitions of right and wrong. Decisions surrounding those laws don't need to be thought out. Other decisions, such as which job to take or which opportunity to accept, are different. For those we do need to pray, see what the Bible says, and discern the Holy Spirit's guidance. Yet, always remember that as long as we are seeking God's kingdom first and living for Christ in a way that will honor Him, we are in His will!

Remember, though, that God has placed special guidance for us in His Word. The following two passages are a few of the many in the Bible that show God's will for Christians.

Hebrews 13:16 (page 929)

Luke 6:31,36 (page 786)

If we know of someone in need, God tells us to help them. We don't have to pray about that. What we should pray about, however, is *how* He wants us to help them. Should we write a check, buy them groceries, fix their car, or clean their house? Wait for the Holy Spirit to inspire you in how to follow God's will.

What is a way God has led you to follow His will through the inspiration of the Holy Spirit?

As we approach the end of the wonderful book of Ruth, in its final verses we see the full result of God's will and measure of His blessing revealed. Read Ruth 4:13-22 (page 210).

This beautifully reflects the purpose of a family redeemer. Naomi was given back her life through Boaz's redeeming her land and marrying her daughter-in-law. Christ has given back our lives by paying for our sins and redeeming us through His death on the cross.

Imagine going from being a barren, destitute, widowed alien to a wealthy, respected woman of influence—and most wondrous of all—a mother! Imagine Ruth's happiness to find herself pregnant after years of barrenness. And look at Naomi! Joy almost drips from the words of verse 16. At long last, she is holding in her arms a precious grandson.

In spite of Naomi's wandering heart, God kept working to make sure she arrived at this point in time. And just look at the genealogy of this baby. Naomi's great-great-grandson became Israel's greatest king!

How did God describe David when He chose him to be king? Read Acts 13:22 (page 842).

Boaz's and Ruth's faithfulness to God carried down through the generations. King David followed God with great devotion. And God blessed David mightily. Obedience to God pleases Him.

To live your life in His will is an ongoing adventure. Your decision to follow in His footprints unleashes His power, wisdom, and love in your life, so that even when the worst happens, you will not be broken. Just as God worked through Naomi and Ruth's devastating circumstances to transform their unbearable pain into deep joy, God can work in your life. It all starts when you begin a relationship with Him and surrender your life to Him.

In chapter 1 you wrote down a decision you had to make. How has this study clarified the issue for you?

Think of all the people who were blessed as a result of God's working in Ruth's life. Every person since is a recipient of those blessings because it was through Ruth that God perpetuated the earthly lineage that would bring Jesus to this earth to be our Savior.

Now think of Naomi's life. In spite of her failures and lack of faith, God kept drawing her to Him—using her, even in the midst of her darkest, most faithless days to introduce Ruth to Him.

God loves you and will continue to pursue you, even in your most faithless days. The question is, though, how will you pursue Him back?

―――――― *Personal Reflection and Application* ――――――

From this chapter,

I see...

I believe...

I will...

Prayer

Lord, you are my sun and my shield. You give me grace and glory. You will withhold no good thing from me when I do what is right. Teach me your ways, O Lord, that I may live according to your truth! Grant me purity of heart, so that I may honor you. You are a God of compassion and mercy, slow to get angry and filled with unfailing love and faithfulness (Psalm 84:11, page 452, and Psalm 86:11,15, page 453).

Thoughts, Notes, and Prayer Requests

_____

_____

_____

_____

_____

_____

_____

_____

_____

_____

_____

_____

_____

_____

_____

_____

_____

_____

_____

_____

_____

_____

Journal Pages

Know God

It does not matter what has happened in your past. No matter what you've done, no matter how you've lived your life,

God is personally interested in you right now.
He cares about you.

God understands your frustration, your loneliness, your heartaches. He wants each of us to come to Him, to know Him personally.

God is so rich in mercy, and he loved us so much, that even
though we were dead because of our sins, he gave us
life when he raised Christ from the dead.
(It is only by God's grace that you have been saved!)

—*Ephesians 2:4-5 (page 895)*

God loves you.

He created you in His image. His desire is to be in relationship with you. He wants you to belong to Him.

Sadly, our sin gets in the way. It separates us from God, and without Him we are dead in our spirits. There is nothing we can do to close that gap. There is nothing we can do to give ourselves life. No matter how well we may behave.

But God loves us so much He made a way to eliminate that gap and give us new life, His kind of life—to restore the relationship. His love for us is so great, so tremendous, that He sent Jesus Christ, His only Son, to earth to live, and then die—filling the gap and taking the punishment we deserve for refusing God's ways.

God made Christ, who never sinned,
to be the offering for our sin, so that we could
be made right with God through Christ.

—*2 Corinthians 5:21 (page 884)*

Jesus Christ, God's Son, not only died to pay the penalty for your sin, but He conquered death when He rose from the grave. He is ready to share His life with you.

Christ reconciles us to God. Jesus is alive today.
He will give you a new beginning and a newly created life
when you surrender control of your life to Him.

Anyone who belongs to Christ has become a new
person. The old life is gone; a new life has begun!

—*2 Corinthians 5:17 (page 884)*

How do you begin this new life? You need to realize

...the necessity of repenting from sin and turning to
God, and of having faith in our Lord Jesus.

—*Acts 20:21 (page 849)*

Agree with God about your sins and believe that Jesus came to save you, that He is your Savior and Lord. Ask Him to lead your life.

God loved the world so much that he gave his
one and only Son, so that everyone who believes in him
will not perish but have eternal life.
God sent his Son into the world not to judge the
world, but to save the world through him.

—*John 3:16-17 (page 811)*

Pray something like this:

Jesus, I do believe you are the Son of God and that you died on the cross to pay the penalty for my sin. I agree with you about my sin and I want to live a life that pleases you. Enter my life as my Savior and Lord.

I want to follow you and make you the leader of my life.

Thank you for your gift of eternal life and for the Holy Spirit, who has now come to live in me. I ask this in your name. Amen.

God puts His Spirit inside you, who enables you to live a life pleasing to Him. He gives you new life that will never die, that will last forever—eternally.

When you surrender your life to Jesus Christ, you are making the most important decision of your life. Stonecroft would like to offer you a free download of *A New Beginning*, a short Bible study that will help you as you begin your new life in Christ. Go to **stonecroft.org/ newbeginning**.

If you'd like to talk with someone right now about this prayer, call **1.888.NEED.HIM**.

Who Is Stonecroft?

Connecting women with God, each other,
and their communities

E very day Stonecroft communicates the Gospel in meaningful
ways. Whether through a speaker sharing her transformational
story, or side by side in a ministry service project, the Gospel of
Jesus Christ goes forward. In one-on-one conversations with a long-
term friend, and through well-developed online and print resources,
the Gospel of Jesus Christ goes forward.

For nearly 75 years, we've been introducing women to Jesus Christ
and training them to share His Good News with others.

Stonecroft understands and appreciates the influence of one woman's life. When you reach her, you touch everyone she knows—her
family, friends, neighbors, and co-workers. The real Truth of the Gospel brings real redemption into real lives.

Our life-changing, faith-building community resources include:

- ***Stonecroft Bible and Book Studies***—both topical and
  traditional chapter-by-chapter studies. Stonecroft studies
  are designed for those in small groups—those who know
  Christ and those who do not yet know Him—to simply
  yet profoundly discover God's Word together.

- ***Outreach Events and Service Activities***—set the stage
  for women to be encouraged and equipped to hear and
  share the Gospel with their communities. Whether in a

large venue, workshop, or small-group setting, women are prepared to serve their communities with the love of Christ.

- **Small-Group Studies for Christians**—these studies engage believers in God's heart for those who do not know Him. Our most recent, the Aware series, includes *Aware, Belong,* and *Call.*

- **Stonecroft Life Publications**—clearly explain the Gospel through stories of people whose lives have been transformed by Jesus Christ.

- **Stonecroft Prayer**—foundational for everything we do, prayer groups, materials, and training set the focus on our reliance on God for all ministry and to share the Gospel.

- **Stonecroft's Website**—stonecroft.org—offering fresh content daily to equip and encourage you.

Dedicated and enthusiastic Stonecroft staff serve you via Divisional Field Directors stationed across the United States, and a Home Office team overseeing the leadership of tens of thousands of dedicated volunteers worldwide.

Your life matters. Join us today to impact your communities with the Gospel of Jesus Christ. Become involved with Stonecroft.

To get started, visit us at **stonecroft.org** or contact us via **connections@stonecroft.org** or **800.525.8627**.

STONECROFT
stonecroft.org

Books for Further Study

Block, Daniel I. *Judges, Ruth,* New American Commentary, vol. 6. Nashville, TN: Broadman & Holman, 1999.

Elliot, Elisabeth. *God's Guidance: Finding His Will for Your Life.* Grand Rapids, MI: Fleming H. Revell, 2006.

Friesen, Garry, and J. Robin Maxson. *Decision Making and the Will of God.* Colorado Springs, CO: Multnomah Books, 2004.

Guinness, Os. *The Call.* Nashville, TN: Thomas Nelson, 2003.

James, Carolyn Custis. *The Gospel of Ruth.* Grand Rapids, MI: Zondervan, 2008.

McVey, Steve. *Walking in the Will of God.* Eugene, OR: Harvest House Publishers, 2009.

Packer, J.I. *Decisions: Finding God's Will.* Downers Grove, IL: InterVarsity Press, 1996.

Shirer, Priscilla. *Discerning the Voice of God: How to Recognize When God Is Speaking.* Chicago: Moody Publishers, 2012.

Stonecroft Resources

Stonecroft Bible Studies make the Word of God accessible to everyone. These studies allow small groups to discover the adventure of a personal relationship with God and introduce others to God's unlimited love, grace, forgiveness, and power. To learn more, visit **stonecroft.org/biblestudies**.

Who Is Jesus? (6 chapters)
He was a rebel against the status quo. The religious community viewed Him as a threat. The helpless and outcast considered Him a friend. Explore the life and teachings of Jesus—this rebel with a cause who challenges us today to a life of radical faith.

What Is God Like? (6 chapters)
What is God like? Is He just a higher power? Has He created us and left us on our own? Where is He when things don't make sense? Discover what the Bible tells us about God and how we can know Him in a life-transforming way.

Who Is the Holy Spirit? (6 chapters)
Are you living up to the full life that God wants for you? Learn about the Holy Spirit, our Helper and power source for everyday living, who works in perfect harmony with God the Father and Jesus the Son.

Connecting with God (8 chapters)
Prayer is our heart-to-heart communication with our heavenly Father. This study examines the purpose, power, and elements of prayer, sharing biblical principles for effective prayer.

Today I Pray

When we bow before God on behalf of someone who doesn't yet know of His saving work, of His great love in sending His Son Jesus, of His mercy and goodness, we enter into a work that has eternal impact. Stonecroft designed *Today I Pray* as a 30-day intercessory prayer commitment that you may use to focus your prayers on behalf of a specific person, or to pray for many— because your prayers are powerful and important!

Prayer Worth Repeating (15 devotions)

There is no place where your prayers to the one and only God cannot penetrate, no circumstance prayers cannot impact. As the mother of adult children, your greatest influence into their lives is through prayer. *Prayer Worth Repeating* is a devotional prayer guide designed to focus your prayers and encourage you to trust God more deeply as He works in the lives of your adult children.

Pray & Play Devotional (12 devotions)

It's playgroup with a purpose! Plus Mom tips. For details on starting a Pray & Play group, visit **stonecroft.org/prayandplay** or call **800.525.8627**.

Prayer Journal

A practical resource to strengthen your prayer life, this booklet includes an introductory section about the importance of prayer, the basic elements of prayer and a clear Gospel presentation, as well as 40 pages of journaling your prayer requests and God's answers.

Prayer—Talking with God

This booklet provides insight and biblical principles to help you establish a stronger, more effective prayer life.

Aware (5 lessons)

Making Jesus known every day starts when we are *Aware* of those around us. This dynamic Stonecroft Small Group Bible Study about "Always Watching and Responding with Encouragement" equips and engages people in the initial steps to the joys of evangelism.

Belong (6 lessons)

For many in today's culture, the desire to belong is often part of their journey to believe. *Belong* explores how we can follow in Jesus' footsteps—and walk with others on their journey to belong.

Call (7 lessons)

Every day we meet people without Christ. That is God's intention.

He wants His people to initiate and build friendships. He wants us together. *Call* helps us take a closer look at how God makes Himself known through our relationships with those around us.

Discover together God's clear calling for you and those near to you.

These and many more Stonecroft resources are available to you.

Order today to impact your communities with the
Gospel of Jesus Christ.
Simply visit **stonecroft.org/store** to get started.

If you have been encouraged and brought closer to God by this study, please consider giving a gift to Stonecroft so that others can experience life change as well. You can find information about giving online at **stonecroft.org.** (Click on the "Donate" tab.)

If you'd like to give via telephone, please contact us at **800.525.8627.** Or you can mail your gift to

Stonecroft
PO Box 9609
Kansas City, MO 64134-0609

STONECROFT

PO Box 9609, Kansas City, MO 64134-0609
Telephone: 816.763.7800 | 800.525.8627
E-mail: connections@stonecroft.org | stonecroft.org

Abundant Life Bible
New Living Translation Holy Bible

Experience the presence of God in everyday life

Stonecroft is pleased to partner with Tyndale to offer the New Living Translation Holy Bible as the companion for our newly released Stonecroft Bible Studies.

The New Living Translation translators set out to render the message of the original Scripture language texts into clear, contemporary English. In this *translation*, scholars kept the concerns of both formal-equivalence and dynamic-equivalence in mind. Their goal was a Bible that is faithful to the ancient texts and eminently readable. The result is a translation that is both accurate and powerful.

TRUTH MADE CLEAR

Features of the Abundant Life Bible

- Features are easy-to-use and written for people who don't yet know Jesus Christ personally.
- Unequaled clarity and accuracy
- Dictionary included
- Concordance included
- Old Testament included

- Introductory notes on important abundant life topics such as:
  - Gospel presentation
  - Joy
  - Peace
  - Practical guidance
  - Life's tough issues
  - Prayer
- Insights from a relationship with Jesus Christ.
- Ideal Scripture text for those not familiar with the Bible!

Tyndale House Publishers

To order: stonecroft.org/store
800.525.8627

 STONECROFT
stonecroft.org/SBS

Notes

||||||||||||||||||||||||

1. Lisa Kepner, "Yates, Ira Griffith, Jr.," Handbook of Texas Online, accessed 9/6/12, www.tshaonline.org/handbook/online/articles/fyazp. Published by the Texas State Historical Association.

2. Carolyn Custis James, *The Gospel of Ruth* (Grand Rapids, MI: Zondervan, 2008), p. 44. Stonecroft wishes to thank Ms. James for the inspiration we have gained from her book for *Living in God's Will*.

3. Viktor E. Frankl, *Man's Search for Meaning* (Boston: Beacon Press, 1959).

4. James, p. 98.

5. Ingrid Betancourt, *Even Silence Has an End* (New York: Penguin Press, 2010).

6. Daniel I. Block, *Judges, Ruth*, New American Commentary 6. (Nashville, TN: Broadman & Holman, 1999), pp. 609-610.

7. James, p. 147.

8. James, p. 117.